CANADA
The Scenic Land

CANADA
The Scenic Land

Richard T. Wright and Stan Garrod

Published by

Whitecap Books Ltd.,
1615 Venables Street,
Vancouver, B.C.,
V5L 2H1

ISBN 0-920620-28-0
Printed in Canada

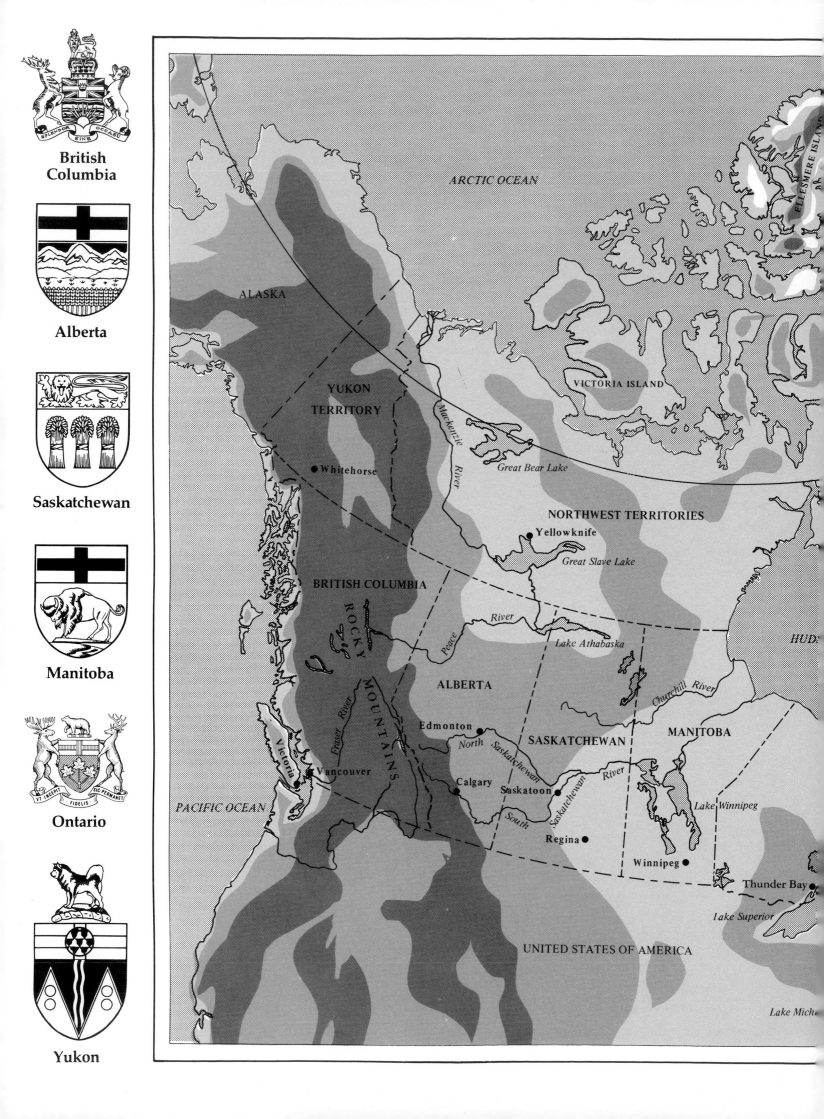

British
Columbia

Alberta

Saskatchewan

Manitoba

Ontario

Yukon

ARCTIC OCEAN

ELLESMERE ISLAND

ALASKA

YUKON
TERRITORY

● Whitehorse

VICTORIA ISLAND

Mackenzie River

Great Bear Lake

NORTHWEST TERRITORIES

● Yellowknife

Great Slave Lake

BRITISH COLUMBIA

ROCKY MOUNTAINS

River

Peace

Lake Athabaska

ALBERTA

Churchill River

MANITOBA

HUD:

Fraser River

Edmonton ●

North Saskatchewan

SASKATCHEWAN

Victoria

Vancouver ●

Calgary ●

Saskatoon ●

Saskatchewan River

Lake Winnipeg

PACIFIC OCEAN

South

Regina ●

Winnipeg ●

Thunder Bay ●

Lake Superior

UNITED STATES OF AMERICA

Lake Mich.

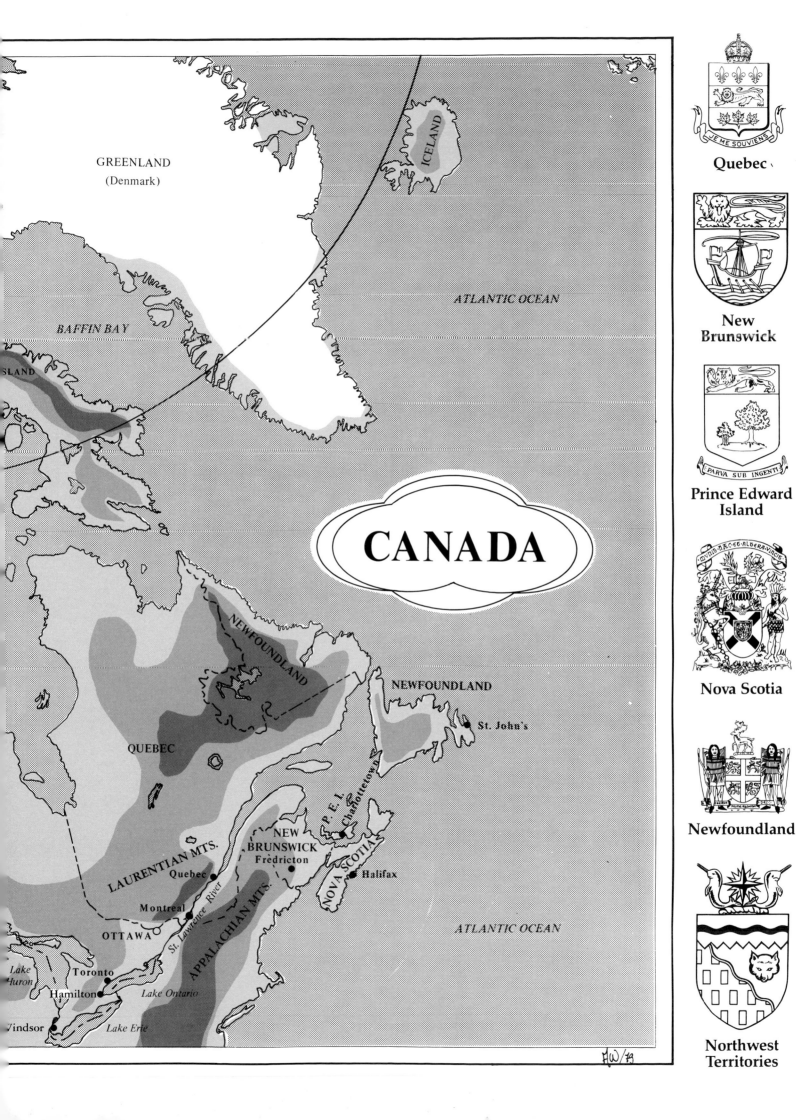

GREENLAND
(Denmark)

ICELAND

ATLANTIC OCEAN

BAFFIN BAY

ISLAND

CANADA

NEWFOUNDLAND

NEWFOUNDLAND

St. John's

QUEBEC

LAURENTIAN MTS.

P.E.I.
Charlottetown

NEW
BRUNSWICK
Frèdricton

Quebec

NOVA SCOTIA

Halifax

Montreal

St. Lawrence River

APPALACHIAN MTS.

OTTAWA

ATLANTIC OCEAN

Lake
Huron

Toronto

Hamilton

Lake Ontario

Windsor

Lake Erie

Quebec

New
Brunswick

Prince Edward
Island

Nova Scotia

Newfoundland

Northwest
Territories

Credits

Designed by
Michael Burch

Edited by
J. Elaine Jones

Illustrations by
Barb Wood

Printed and bound by
**D. W. Friesen & Sons Ltd.
Altona, Manitoba**

Color separations by
**Tri-Scan Graphics
Vancouver, B.C.**

———————————

This book is financially assisted
by the Government of British Columbia
through the B.C. Cultural Fund.

The Photographers

We would like to acknowledge the following
photographers for their contribution to
this book.

J. A. Kraulis — Page 10, 11, 12 [below], 13, 14,
16 and 17, 18, 19 [above], 22 [below], 23, 24, 33,
34, 35, 42, 43 [below], 44, 45, 46, 47, 48, 57, 58,
59 [below], 60, 61, 62, 66 [above], 67 [below], 69,
70, 71, 72, 81, 82, 84, 85, 86, 91, 92, 93, 95, 96.

Bob Herger — Page 43 [above], 59 [above],
88 and 89, 90.

Ed Gifford — Page 66 [below]

Frank Mayrs — Page 67 [above]

Scott Rowed — Back cover, page 12 [above], 20, 21, 36, 37, 83.

Duncan McDougall — Front cover, page 38,
64 and 65, 68.

Pat Morrow — Pages 19 [below], and 94.

Richard T. Wright — Page 22 [above]

Myron Kozak — Page 15 [above and below]
and page 87 [above and below]

Gérald Perrault — Pages 40 and 41.

This book is distributed in Eastern Canada by
Firefly Books Ltd.
3520 Pharmacy Ave., Unit 1C
Scarborough, Ontario

Introduction

Quebec City

BARB·WOOD.

From the Pacific Ocean prevailing northwesterly winds have swept a ridge of low pressure across the sea to the islands of the west coast. Like the waves that now crash against the shores and race up the fiords of the coast, the gray clouds have caught and hung on the coastal mountains. The ubiquitous sea gulls have come inland with the scent of the salt sea wind. Rain falls from a leaden sky, a fine rain that mists the trees and beads on the end of bare branches and buds of spring. The beads grow, elusive temporal mirors reflecting the west coast environment, but in the mind's eye there are further images, images of Canada, swept east by the wind.

Here is the coast: green, rugged, often storm bound, confusing to the early sailors who searched for the elusive route through to the Atlantic. The clouds lose their moisture to the Coast Mountain Range, and dry winds sweep down the east slopes to where a cowboy rides across the grassland of British Columbia's Chilcotin cattle country, and to where river rafters descend through the deep whitewater filled gorges. Past the historic roadhouses of goldrush days — 87 Mile House, 100 Mile House, 150 Mile House — a semi-trailer and tractor hauls produce along the Cariboo Highway.

Three mountain ranges east, in the Rockies, abundant wildlife roams the protected mountain slopes; mountain sheep and goats, elk, and ursus horribilis, Ol' Griz, the grizzly bear. Skiers carve their downward fall into the winter snow while climbers laboriously ascend similar peaks that reach like fingers to the heavens. Eastward lie the northern parklands, carpeted with vast pine and spruce forests, and the wheatfields of the prairies, dotted with rocking oil pumps, domed churches and monolithic grain elevators. The level plains race eastward, an elemental land of earth and sky.

To the north, beyond the wheat fields, lie the subarctic forests, a land of light and darkness which stretches north to the pole. In this frozen landscape, an Inuit sits patiently beside a hole in the ice, harpoon in hand, waiting for a seal to surface and breathe his last. Nearby are his rifle and snowmobile. In Whitehorse a Yukoner mushes his dogs toward the finish line, taking part in a recreation grown from the skill and transportation method used for centuries. An oil drilling rig sits stolidly in the Beaufort Sea, scant kilometres from an archaeological site that shows evidence of European trading and settlement centuries earlier than was ever imagined. A peregrine falcon, one of the last of his kind, soars high over a river basin, dives for a vole and misses, then veers away from the broad new road that curves north through the Yukon to the high Arctic.

The Canadian Shield, scraped and scoured by the glaciers that have retreated northward, pockmarked with small lakes, dotted with timber, stretches east from the prairies almost to the St. Lawrence River. In Ontario's Quetico Provincial Park a canoeist traces the route of the early voyageurs and merchants who travelled these tea colored waters in search of furs. Mines mark the northern shield: nickle, uranium, cobalt and iron ore mines to feed the industries of Ontario.

There are images of Kensington market, Toronto's city hall, Hamilton steel mills, a southern Ontario farm, tobacco fields and canals. Here are the parliament buildings in Ottawa, the snow covered Gatineau Mountains and the Rideau Canal speckled with ice-skaters. In St. Jean Port Joli there is a wood carver and in Quebec City the street artists, the Plains of Abraham and the wall of an old city. The sun is shining on Bras d'Or Lake and catching the spires of the King's Gate at Fortress Louisburg. There are waves from the Atlantic washing the red shores of Prince Edward Island, where a farmer sits on the oven door, talking of crops and his family. And in Newfoundland there is L'Anse aux Meadows, where Vikings landed and tried to settle and there are the outports, small and isolated communities of hardy fishermen.

The images cease, and from the stillness emerge the sounds of Canada. There is the cry of the black-backed gulls on the east coast, a church bell in New Brunswick, the sound of a train whistle in the vast loneliness of the prairies, swept away by the wind, an exploration chopper whirling across the northern ice. There is the call of the loon on a wilderness lake, the soft dip of a canoe paddle, a fiddle and the rhythm of the spoons, the pipes in a small village, the harmony of church choirs across the land, waves on the east shore and waves on the west shore. There is the grind and clash of ice going out in the spring, the sound of icebergs turning over and waves lapping their edges. Horns sound in Montreal streets, trolleys clang in Toronto. There are the sounds of timber falling, rivers running, dams being built, rock being drilled, ships being docked, cows being milked and crops being harvested . . . and there is the sound of rain softly falling on the west coast, muffled by cedar boughs.

The rain drops bead, grow larger and fall, their images melding, their individuality adding to the streams that flow across the land and through this country.

These are pictures of a vast land. From where the morning sun casts orange light on the fishnets and lobster pots of the east coast to where it bounces off the west coast sands of Long Beach in the evening is a distance of 6,000 kilometres. From the border with the United States at the 49th parallel it stretches 4500 kilometres to the North Pole. In all, this land of contrasts encompasses nearly 10 million square kilometres. It is larger than the United States, larger than China; it is the second largest nation in the world, exceeded in area only by the Soviet Union. This is Canada.

Percé Rock on the Gaspé peninsula, Quebec.

Mount Maxwell from inside the Kaskawulsh Glacier, Yukon.

Helicopter skiing in the Monashees, British Columbia.

Glacier Peak and Mount Ringrose, Yoho National Park.

Mary Lake and Lake O'Hara, Yoho National Park.

The Consolation Lakes from Mount Temple, Banff National Park.

Mount Asgard and the Caribou Glacier, Baffin Island.

Eskimo and Kayak, Northwest Territories.

Whistling Swans near the Beaufort Sea.

Following pages: St. Mary's Alpine Park, British Columbia.

Storm over the Prairies near Medicine Hat, Alberta.

Ski touring in rural Quebec.

Golden autumn, Huntsville, Ontario.

Summer canoe expedition on the Peel River in the Yukon.

Frosty trees at Vermillion Pass, Alberta.

Ski mountaineering, the Selkirk Mountains, British Columbia.

'Green Gables', Prince Edward Island.

The 'Maid of the Mist', Niagara Falls, Ontario.

The lighthouse at Peggy's Cove, Nova Scotia.

The brilliant fall color of a maple in eastern Canada.

Caledon area, Ontario

BARB WOOD

Canada: The Land

Any description of Canada centres around the physical reality of the land: its size, scope and diversity. One of its most obvious features is the large tracts of wilderness territory. Its vast area and northern location, with a sometimes forbidding climate, have ensured that much of this beautiful country is unpopulated. Richly endowed with natural resources, Canada has attracted settlers and investors from all over the world. Yet it remains a land barely touched; only 10% of it is inhabited.

Despite being a largely urban people, Canadians are closely tied to the land. The spirit of adventure, freedom, challenge and the harsh realities of nature contribute in an indefinable way to the Canadian identity. More practically, the people here benefit very visibly from the land's rich resources. They reap its harvests of grain and fruit, build with its abundant forests, extract its oil and minerals, venture into its bordering seas for the bounty of the ocean and enjoy the wide variety of recreational opportunities which the land provides.

Canadian landscapes form a spectrum which spans semi-desert, rain forest and a perpetually frozen land of ice. The country is bordered by three separate oceans, boasts a number and variety of mountain ranges and great fertile plains. Because of this complexity and variety, the land defies easy description.

Writers, artists and photographers have long struggled to capture the land in images. It has been described as a land which is always an unknown quantity, where mystery lies just over the rim of the hills or beyond the bend in the river. It has been called a land as elusive as the fading cry of a wolf in the still Arctic night air, or the call of a loon vanishing into the mist of a wilderness lake. It has been described in musical terms: the endless wide-horizoned prairies pictured as Bach fugues, the Rockies as colossal symphonies of Wagnerian proportions, the rivers as laughing, dancing melodies. No one description ever captures the essence of Canada in all its complexity.

Out of this complex interplay of elements, a pattern emerges. Canada's landscapes may be sorted into six great landform regions, each with marked physical features. Canada's northern location has left a distinct stamp on the character of the country, so it is perhaps appropriate to begin with Canada's northernmost region, the high Arctic.

Within the Canadian Arctic there is the same diversity of landforms, from towering mountains to gentle plains, that marks the rest of Canada. But the common factor in the north is the extent to which these differing areas are literally frozen into a common landscape. No region of the country is so dominated by climate as Canada's Arctic, so subject to the power of cold and ice.

In the last 1,000,000 years, 97% of Canada's surface has been covered by glacial ice; 17,000 years ago most of Canada was still covered by glaciers during the last great ice-age. Today, the Canadian Arctic is all that remains of that great empire of ice. Most of the glaciers that covered the region have gone. Only a few ice caps remain, on Alex Heiberg, Baffin, Devon, and Ellesmere Islands, relics of the glaciers that once covered all of the land. But only a few centimetres below the surface of the Arctic landscape an icy legacy remains.

Permafrost, a layer of ice reaching as many as 30 or more metres below the surface of the earth, is permanently frozen ground. This permafrost layer extends throughout the Arctic region; its southernmost extension marks the boundary of the Arctic.

The frozen lands of the Arctic have been called many things by those who have known them. The Inuit call their home the 'Land of No Tomorrows'. Later visitors called it 'The White Hell' and 'The Ultimate Desolation'. Today, with the promise of oil, gas and other riches lying beneath the permafrost, others are calling the Arctic 'Canada's Last Frontier'.

The Arctic is also known as the 'Land of the Midnight Sun', for north of the Arctic Circle, summer nights and days blend into one another. There is a strange magic to the Arctic summer night. On the horizon, the sun appears to just touch the earth. It seems to stand motionless; then it rises once more instead of disappearing below the horizon.

There is great beauty in the Arctic, Permafrost is one of nature's most accomplished visual designers, breaking the icy surface into eye-catching geometric patterns: ovals, circles, stripes and polygons. Perhaps the most striking of these patterned areas when seen from the air are the tundra polygons, great crystal cells 50 or more metres across.

Some are as regular and precise as chessboards or prairie wheatfields; others look like the markings on a giant turtle's back.

In winter the Arctic is windswept and often bleak. Drifting snow and ice shape a surreal landscape where distinction between earth and ocean and between hill and plain are blurred. Yet spring thaw and the brief Arctic summer reveal beauty and life that the harshest winter cannot suppress. Each year, amid the windswept dunes, the marshy soil and the ice-shattered rocks, the tundra comes alive with bright flowers and verdant shrubs.

South of the Arctic, in a great weathered stone arc sweeping from northern British Columbia to Newfoundland, lies the Canadian Shield. These ancient rocks make up the low hills of the Shield, the oldest exposed rock on the earth's surface, and all that remains of a once towering mountain range.

A billion years ago and more, all there was to North America was a rocky ridge in the sea. Where the Shield lies today, there was a high and rugged mountain range. Higher than the Rocky Mountains of today, it was surrounded by an ancient sea.

Earthquakes rocked this land, shattering rocks as the mountains rose above the sea. Deep in the heart of the earth, the ancient elemental fire had not cooled. Magma, hot liquid rock, flowed into cracks in the shattered mountains. As it flowed, the magma carried gold, silver, lead, zinc, copper and many other minerals up from the heart of the earth's core.

During the millions of years that followed, the mountains were slowly worn away by erosion. Ice, snow, heat, wind, and water, working slower than the human eye could ever see, chipped away at the mountains. Rivers and glaciers cut their way through the rock, carrying the mountains piece by piece out to sea where they were deposited as sediment.

Then came the ice ages. Great sheets of ice slowly moved across the land like giant bulldozer blades, leaving a flat landscape of lakes and low rolling hills. In many places, bare rock was left.

Where towering mountains stood, the Canadian Shield now crouched. Exposed too, were the pockets into which the magma had flowed, leaving behind rich deposits of minerals. Thousands of years were to pass before humans would become aware of the treasures left in the Shield by the magma.

Prospectors came, first on foot, then on snowshoes and dogsleds, then by aircraft and highway to the forests of the Canadian Shield. They found not only copper and silver, but also gold, lead, zinc, iron, nickel and platinum. Today the Canadian Shield is one of the world's great mining regions, and the leading producer of many of these important metals.

The thin soils that cover the Canadian Shield and the harsh winters of the region combine to severely limit the potential for agriculture here. But the Shield is extensively covered by forests of evergreen trees. These stands of firs, spruce, larch and pine are so large that this area is sometimes referred to as the Subarctic Forest Region. The forests of the subarctic are the basis of a very valuable lumber industry, with much of the timber being used for pulp and paper products. Many of the world's newspapers are printed on the products of the Canadian Shield.

Forests also dominate the landscape of British Columbia and the Yukon, Canada's Western Mountain region. Three major mountain ranges make up the Western Mountains: The Rocky Mountains, The Coast Mountains, and the Insular Mountains. A series of plateaus, called the Interior Plateau or the Interior Uplands, lies between the Rockies and the Coast Mountains.

The mountains of the west are very young by the standards of geological time. The uplifting, folding, and faulting that shaped these great sedimentary blocks into the Rocky Mountains took place only some 65 million years ago, at a time when the once tall peaks of the Shield had already been worn away by the millennia. In their youth, the Rockies are loftier and more rugged than any other range in Canada because nature's sculptors have not had time enough to give them gentler, less arrogant faces. The highest peak in the Canadian Rockies is Mount Robson at 3954 metres (12,072 feet) and there are many others that exceed 3500 metres.

Older than any work of man, the Canadian Rockies are truly one of the great natural wonders of the world. Thousands of tourists from all over the world come to the Rockies every year, trying to capture the awesome majesty of these great rocks in their cameras, unaware of the poet who said that these mountains make the mind ache with the awareness of its own insignificance. Not everyone comes to capture the Rockies this way. Others try to capture the spirit of the Rockies through experience: climbers, hikers and skiers whose hearts soar like eagles over the mountains as they rise to the challenge, adventure and freedom.

Rarely wider than 100 kilometres, the Rocky Mountains were long a barrier blocking the way to Canada's Pacific coast. There are no rivers that traverse these awesome mountains, no easy route across the ridges. The same peaks that thrill climbers and travellers, and inspire poets and painters were massive stumbling blocks to the explorers and to engineers who tried to build roads and railways through the few mountain passes leading westward to the sea.

Along Canada's west coast, the mountains rise straight out of the sea. They block the winds, bringing the ever present rains that water the great evergreen forests and feed a multitude of streams and rivers. These coast mountains are older than the Rockies, and their features are more rounded and gentle. But these are also mountains of majestic grandeur and spectacular scenery. The tallest peak in the Coast Range, Mount Waddington, at 4016 metres (13,260 feet) is taller than any in the Rockies.

Glacial ice and rain-fed rivers have combined to shape the distinctive landscape of the British Columbia coast. Many fiords, long arms of the sea, were sculpted by glaciers flowing down river valleys to the ocean. They run far inland, giving British Columbia a coastline that is many thousands of kilometres long and possessed of great scenic beauty. Giant Douglas firs and imposing red cedars line the mountain slopes to the water's edge.

There is a special beauty to the coast mountains at dusk on a summer or fall evening. The lines of hills and inlets stand in soft parallel rows, each a different pastel shade of twilight, suggested rather than defined, like a Chinese watercolor deftly brushed onto silk, changing color with the seconds as the sun sets over the Pacific.

The last rays of the western sunset fall on the Insular Mountains of Vancouver Island and the Queen Charlotte Islands. These islands are formed of mountain ranges that rise from the seabed, showing only their tops. To the north, the island mountains continue inland into the Yukon and northwestern British Columbia. Here they become the St. Elias Range, remote, ice-capped peaks which few Canadians have ever seen. The tallest peak in Canada, Mount Logan (5950 metres, 19,850 feet), is located here, as is the tallest mountain in British Columbia, Mount Fairweather (4663 metres, 15,300 feet). Mount Logan is located in beautiful Kluane National Park, one of Canada's finest wilderness parks.

Canada's western mountains are studded with pockets of riches; huge deposits of coal, lead, zinc, copper, asbestos, silver, and gold have been found in this region and the many mines of the area contribute greatly to Canada's economy. Little of the land is well-suited to agriculture except for that along the rivers and lakes. Two great rivers rise in the Rockies, the Columbia and the Fraser, and fertile soils are found along their floodplains. The land of the Fraser Valley is among the most fertile in Canada; there are many highly productive farms in this beautiful mountain-walled valley that runs to the sea. Cattle graze the Interior Plateau and irrigated fruit farms line the lakes of the Okanagan Valley, giving the region a diversified agricultural economy despite its limited amount of farm land.

Great trees can grow where crops can't, and this is very true of the Western Mountains. The lower slopes are covered by huge stands of timber. The trees are largest along the Pacific, where rainfall is heaviest, but forests cover nearly all of the region. The large trees of the coast are taken to sawmills and turned into high quality lumber for shipment around the world. The smaller trees of the interior forests are used both for lumber and for pulp and paper making. The forest industry dominates the economy of the Western Mountain region.

Trees once covered much of the Prairie Region, Canada's youngest geographic zone, lying to the east of the Rocky Mountains, but today grasslands and great fields of wheat dominate the central plains of Alberta, Saskatchewan, and southern Manitoba. North of the Saskatchewan River the forests remain, gradually merging with the subarctic forest of the Canadian Shield.

Like the Shield, the landscape of the Prairies has been greatly shaped by glaciation. The great sheets of ice retreated northwards, leaving behind a sweep of flat plains and gently undulating hills. There are many wide deep valleys that were formed by the rivers of melt-water flowing away from the retreating margins of ice. The rivers are gone now; seen from the air these valleys dwarf the insignificant streams that cut their way across the plains. Only the Saskatchewan River system remains as a reminder of what these ancient glacial rivers must have looked like.

Standing on the wide skyskirted prairies, with unbroken fields of golden grain

The Prairies; Robsart, Saskatchewan

stretched out in all directions to the far-distant horizon, and all about and above the cloudless blue dome of heaven, it is possible to believe that the earth is indeed flat and that nothing lies beyond the edges of vision.

And there is the wind, the ever-present, unseen but always heard prairie wind. It is often gentle and caressing, setting rippling waves in motion through the wheatfields. But the wind has many tricks. Turn around on a summer's afternoon and the clear blue sky will be replaced by a solid wall of black. The wheatfields, burnished by the late afternoon light, stand in stark contrast to the towering thunderstorm that sweeps suddenly across the open prairie.

Seeing the prairies rich in the golden fullness of harvest it is hard to imagine that the region was once considered to be a barren, infertile area totally unsuited to cultivation or human habitation. The prairie grasslands were home to millions of bison, great shaggy beasts that were food, shelter, clothing and fuel to the Indian and Metis peoples of the plains. Tough grass cover and low rainfall deterred early farm settlers, but the coming of the railroad and the development of agricultural technology, with hardier seed types, saw productive farms replace the grasslands.

Not all the riches of the prairies lie on the surface. The great pressure of the sheets of glacial ice turned millions of tiny plants and animals into coal, petroleum, and natural gas. Today the prairies provide Canada with most of its oil and gas production from fields in Alberta and Saskatchewan.

The Canadian Shield drives a great wedge between the Prairies and the Great Lakes-St. Lawrence River Lowland region to the east, separating Canada's two richest agricultural areas. Unlike the prairies, which are vast in size, the Great Lakes-St. Lawrence region is the smallest of Canada's physiographic zones. At the same time it is the richest and most densely populated area of Canada, owing in part to being the first area of the country to be settled by Europeans.

Like so much of Canada, this region was greatly shaped by glaciation during the successions of ice ages that have swept across North America. The relief is generally level, with little of the land lying more than 150 metres above sea level; the only marked elevation is along the Niagara escarpment in the western part of the region. Here there are heights approaching 500 metres on the Bruce Peninsula. The dominant physical features of the region are water bodies — the Saint Lawrence River and the Great Lakes: Ontario, Huron and Erie — which form the southern and western boundaries of the area.

In a sense, the region is really two separate lowland regions, one in the St. Lawrence River valley, the other lying along the margins of the Great Lakes. An outcropping of the Canadian Shield just east of Kingston, Ontario divides the two zones with a 50 kilometre wide belt of worn rock called the Frontenac Axis, creating the Thousand Islands at the point where the St. Lawrence rises in Lake Ontario. The Thousand Islands are one of the most beautiful areas of Canada, and a favourite recreational retreat for many residents and visitors.

Unlike the Canadian Shield, glaciation left the Great Lakes-St. Lawrence River lowlands with rich and fertile soils. Temperatures are mild in winter and there is a long, warm, summer growing season, giving the area a very good potential for farming. Forests covered much of the region following the retreat of glacial ice; these included fine dense stands of hardwoods such as oak, maple, elm, beech and ash. When the first European explorers arrived, they found the Indians here to be an agricultural people. Areas had been cleared for crops of corn, squash and beans, and also tobacco.

The first of the European explorers to fully recognize the region's potential for European-style farming was Samuel de Champlain. Champlain was to spend the first third of the seventeenth century struggling to get France to support an agricultural settlement on the banks of the St. Lawrence. On his death bed, he wrote to Cardinal Richelieu in France to press his case, saying "In this country is one of the best rivers in the world, into which many other rivers empty themselves . . . The beauty of these lands cannot be overpraised for the fertility of the soil, the extent of the forests, and the opportunities for hunting and fishing in abundance."

In the end, the French succeeded in establishing a flourishing farming community along the St. Lawrence, only to see it fall to the British. After the American Revolution, Loyalists pushed further up the river, opening up the lands along Lake Ontario and on the Niagara Peninsula to farming and settlement.

The settlements of the region flourished, supported by the products of the rich farmlands and by trade and commerce carried out along the convenient waterways of the St. Lawrence, the Ottawa River, and the Great Lakes. Today the Great Lakes-St. Lawrence Lowlands region is the most densely populated in Canada. Nearly sixty per cent of all Canadians live in this small region, most of them in the two great metropolitan centres, Toronto and Montreal. The forests of hardwood trees are gone now, replaced by the ordered precision of neat family farms and orchards, of large-scale commercial farms, and by the ever-growing cities of Ontario and Quebec.

Canada's easternmost geographic area, the Appalachian-Atlantic region, embraces the Maritime provinces, Newfoundland and the Gaspé Peninsula of Quebec. Running north from the United States, the Appalachian Mountain System is a series of modest, well-weathered peaks and hills that terminate at the Atlantic in a dispersed cluster of peninsulas, gulfs, islands and bays. At its broadest, the Appalachian system is about 600 kilometres wide, extending from the Eastern Townships of Quebec to Cape Breton Island.

Glaciation played a major role in shaping the landscapes of this region, exposing bedrock in places but depositing fertile soils elsewhere. Unfortunately, the fertile areas are small and rocky, limiting agriculture. The most productive land is found in Prince Edward Island, where the characteristic red earth is famous for its potatoes. Good land is also found in the Annapolis Valley of Nova Scotia and elsewhere along the margins of the Bay of Fundy.

Prince Edward Island is the jewel of the region, a tiny island with a mild climate and good agricultural land. When Jacques Cartier first landed on the island in 1534, it was covered in luxurious forests, berry patches and grasslands so appealing that Cartier observed that all it lacked was the nightingale to be paradise. Today the forests are replaced with small family farms. Sandy beaches along the shores attract thousands of visitors every year.

By contrast, very little of Newfoundland, New Brunswick, and Nova Scotia are suitable for farming. Trees cover the mountainside and line the ocean shore. Once the tall, straight pines were cut for masts and spars for the ships of the Royal Navy. In the nineteenth century timber from the region gave rise to a flourishing shipbuilding industry and was also exported to Europe. Today, steel hulls have replaced wooden ships and the forests of Atlantic Canada now form the basis of an important pulp and paper industry.

Another great resource of the Atlantic region lies not on or beneath the land, but in its ocean waters. The rich fisheries of the Grand Banks, the shallow continental shelf that runs 500 kilometres out into the Atlantic Ocean, have long been known to European fishermen who may have been crossing the ocean to catch cod long before Columbus and Cabot made their historic voyages. An early travel guide to Nova Scotia described it as a peninsula entirely surrounded by fish. Cod are still caught in great numbers but other valuable catches such as lobsters and scallops contribute much to the Maritime economy.

The fog shrouded, rocky island of Newfoundland was the first land seen by John Cabot when he reached Canada, but it was many years before permanent settlements were founded by the fishermen who came each year to the cod fisheries off the island. Today fishing is still an important source of livelihood for Newfoundlanders, and hundreds of small fishing villages, known as outports, sit picturesquely on the rocky bluffs of the island's many coves and bays. Newfoundland's island location and a long history as a British colony separate from Canada have led to both a sense of isolation and a fiercely proud independence among Newfoundlanders.

This is a brief glimpse into the vast and complex land which is Canada. From Newfoundland to the west coast islands, and from the border with the United States to its most northern limits, it is immense, rich, varied and above all, challenging. The land has determined to a large extent the history of the nation; with its rich resources it holds the promise for the future.

The City Hall, Kingston, Ontario.

Queen Elizabeth Gardens and the City of Vancouver.

The Toronto skyline at sunset.

Cape Sibley near Thunder Bay, Ontario.

The harbour, Lunenberg, Nova Scotia.

Snowdrops, Glacier Lily, Red Heather, and mushrooms, Jasper National Park, Alberta.

Alpine flowers and mountain falls in the Bugaboos, British Columbia.

Grain elevator, Robsart, Saskatchewan.

Sunflower crop near Altona, Manitoba.

Following pages: Fish weir on the St. Lawrence River, St. Siméon, Quebec.

Near Avonlea, Saskatchewan.

Daisies in the Laurentians, Quebec.

The Fraser Valley, British Columbia.

Near St. Stephen, New Brunswick.

Crab Apples, the Columbia River Valley, British Columbia.

Lobster pots, Salvage, Newfoundland.

Garibaldi Lake, British Columbia.

Johnston Canyon, Banff National Park, Alberta.

The Watchtower, Yoho National Park, British Columbia.

Silver Birch near Lake Nipigon, Ontario.

Canada: The History

Fort Macleod, Alberta

Canada's history doesn't start with Cabot or Cartier. Like Columbus, they were relative latecomers to the New World. The first Europeans to arrive in Canada and to attempt settlement were the Vikings, over 500 years before John Cabot. The Vikings, to their cost, soon discovered that they hadn't been the first to arrive either.

The native people of Canada, whose technology was only slightly inferior, and whose numbers were vastly greater, sent the Viking interlopers home. The native Canadians' ancestors had arrived on this continent from Asia some 30,000 years before. They were well established, with many distinctive cultures, by the time the Europeans stumbled across North America. Only with vastly superior technology, and greater numbers of settlers than the Vikings had, would Europeans be able to dispossess Canada's native peoples from their homelands.

Europe, on the eve of the sixteenth century, had the technology and the numbers required to conquer the native inhabitants. Ironically, however, the Europeans seemed to have forgotten what the Vikings once knew, that Canada existed. The records of the Viking ventures lay forgotten in the Vatican archives.

Fishermen from Bristol and Britany and the Basque whalers most likely knew of the rich catches to be found off the coasts of Newfoundland and Nova Scotia. This knowledge may have made its way around the seaport taverns of western Europe, but it hadn't found its way to the cartographers of the Royal courts of Europe. They were just rediscovering what the Greeks had known many centuries before, that the world was a globe.

This exciting rediscovery of the spherical nature of the earth convinced sailors like Christopher Columbus and John Cabot that the riches of the Indies and Cathay — silks and spices — could be reached by sailing westward across the Atlantic. If they were right, it would mean an end to the long and costly caravan trips over the mountains eastward from Asia Minor.

North America stood in the way of their dreams but the first sailors to seek a westward route to the Indies didn't know that. When they found land, they believed they had reached India after all. Naturally, they referred to the people they met as 'Indians'. Because of their mistake, we still call our native people Indians.

John Cabot, sailing from Bristol, reached the shores of Newfoundland in 1497. He was soon followed by French and Portuguese explorers, men like Jean Denys who in 1506 explored the Atlantic coast of Nova Scotia, Thomas Aubert of Dieppe who explored the same region two years later, and the Corte-Real brothers who explored the coast of Newfoundland and Labrador during the years 1500-1502, claiming those territories for Portugal. The Corte-Reals met Indians wearing European jewelry. One carried a European sword. Clearly, other explorers had been here before.

These voyages of discovery soon began to prove one indisputable fact: Canada was neither China nor India. But its true nature remained unknown. The riches of its cod fishery were by now well known, with fishermen coming from Spain, Portugal, France and England. The market for fish was a large one; Europe's Catholics faced 153 meatless days in the church calendar. By the middle of the sixteenth century, many hundreds of ships were coming each year to the Newfoundland fishery. For many years to come, cod fish would remain Canada's most valuable export.

But what other riches did Canada hold? This was the question the king of France was asking himself in 1530. Spain and Portugal by now controlled all of South and Central America. Dramatic reports were making their way to Paris of the great riches of Peru and Mexico, and of enormous amounts of gold and silver being sent back to Spain from the New World. France wondered if such riches might not also be found in Canada.

The French had not given up on the idea of a westward route to India either. It was widely recognized that Canada was part of a new continent, not of Asia as earlier supposed. But it might be possible that a route around, or through, Canada could exist. France had to find out.

In 1534, Jacques Cartier set sail from St. Malo for Canada. His orders were to find a route to China and to find gold and other riches. Both were to elude Cartier. What appeared to be a westward route to Asia turned out to be the St. Lawrence River whose Lachine Rapids blocked his progress at Montreal. There were no gold and silver mines either, but Cartier did find riches in the form of fine furs offered in trade by the Indians he met. Both the river and the furs were to greatly affect the history of Canada, leading to westward exploration and eventual settlement of the interior of the country.

Cartier and his men discovered something else: the harshness of the Canadian winter. On his second voyage in 1535, Cartier was forced to spend the winter at Hochelaga, now Quebec City, after reaching Mont Royal and the Lachine Rapids. There scurvy, the plague of sixteenth century sailors, struck his crew. By February fewer than 10 men out of 110 remained healthy; 25 had died already. Prayers to the virgin brought no relief. It took an Indian cure to return the sailors to health. Evergreen twigs boiled in water made a healing drink that brought them the vitamin C they needed to cure the scurvy.

In a twisted act of gratitude, Cartier kidnapped the Indian chief Donnacona and four of his men. All of the Indian victims died in France, earning Cartier and the French the confirmed hatred of the Iroquois.

Disastrous though it may have been, Cartier's exploration of the St. Lawrence River area had two important results. Out of the visit came Canada's name; the Indians called their villages 'kanata' and Cartier appears to have understood this to be the name 'Canada'. All maps from his voyage onward include the name Canada. And, as a result of Cartier's voyages, the great French fur trade in Canada began.

The remainder of the sixteenth century saw French ships making regular visits to the St. Lawrence to trade for furs. A trading post was established at Tadoussac, just east of Quebec, but no attempt was made to settle or colonize the region until Samuel de Champlain arrived at Quebec in 1609.

Champlain's first visit to Canada was made in 1604 and the following year he participated in the founding of Port Royal, in Nova Scotia, which was the beginning of continuous European settlement in Canada. Champlain's explorations took him away from Port Royal, never to return. Instead, he would spend the next 30 years of his life trying to establish a prosperous French farming colony along the St. Lawrence River. Champlain recognized the growing strength of the English and Dutch colonies to the south and urged the king of France to create a secure settlement to protect French fur-trading interests in Canada. In his attempts to protect the fur trade, Champlain sided with the Hurons against the Iroquois, bringing European weapons and methods of warfare to native conflicts. At his death on Christmas Day, 1635, one hundred years to the day after Cartier had celebrated the first European Christmas in Quebec, Champlain's dream of a prosperous and secure French colony in Canada was not fulfilled, but the roots of the French Canadian community had been established.

The fur trade, not farming, continued to dominate French interest in Canada. The English, aided by two French traders, Radisson and Groselliers, entered into the race for Canadian furs with the establishment of the Hudson's Bay Company in 1670. Competition for control of this valuable resource would lead to war between England and France in Canada.

The conflict first began in Acadia, where a French colony had struggled, then prospered following the founding of Port Royal. The Acadians, hardy Norman and Breton folk, had dyked and drained the salt marshes along the Bay of Fundy. Their farms were highly productive and their numbers grew quickly. The English quickly recognized the strategic importance of Acadia in controlling both the approaches to the St. Lawrence and the cod fishing grounds off the coast. Throughout the sixteenth and seventeenth centuries, New Englanders and English freebooters raided Acadia, and the colony traded hands several times.

To protect Acadia and the approaches to the St. Lawrence, the French built a great stone fortress on Cape Breton Island. The fortress, named Louisburg after the king of France, was the scene of a great seige and battle in 1745, but was returned to France in 1748. The French had to surrender much of their control over Acadia, however, and the following year the military and naval garrison town of Halifax was begun only a few hundred kilometres away. It was from Halifax in 1758 that the last great attack on Louisburg by British forces was launched, leading to the surrender of the fortress.

The fall of Louisburg paved the way for the final British assault on the heartland of New France. The following year, a force of ships and soldiers under the command of General James Wolfe made its way up the St. Lawrence to Quebec, terrorizing the civilian population of the area and burning fishing villages en route. Wolfe's blitzkreig greatly weakened the morale of New France.

The decisive battle of the struggle for control over Canada came just outside Quebec City, on the Plains of Abraham, on September 12, 1759. Despite the heroic myths that have surrounded the Battle of the Plains of Abraham, the contest was a tragedy of errors between two stubborn and egotistical men, Wolfe and Louis-Joseph Montcalm, the commander of the troops defending Quebec. That day the British slipped up the bluffs onto the Plains of Abraham unnoticed, using a difficult back way. Once on the Plains, they were discovered. Their position was vulnerable, for they still had to cross open land to attack the citadel. Montcalm had only to wait and defend his secure position with his superior numbers. Instead, he chose to attack, charging directly into the muskets of the British without waiting for his reserves and reinforcements to be brought to the battlefield. Had Montcalm waited three hours, Canada's history might have been different. Instead, when the smoke of battle cleared, both Wolfe and Montcalm lay dead, and the fall of New France was virtually complete.

Once in control of the Quebec colony, the British acted with foresight, ensuring the religion, language and traditional rights of the French in Canada. When the American Revolution began in 1775, the people of Quebec were invited to join. The Americans thought that the conquered French Canadians would be eager to throw off the recently imposed mantle of British rule, but the Americans would not guarantee religion and language rights. As a result, the Quebec colony did not join the rebellion, despite the support of some British merchants for the American uprising.

The American Revolution saw many families and communities divided over support for the Revolution. Those who did not back the rebellion were called Loyalists; after the defeat of the British many of the Loyalists fled from the new United States to Canada, settling in the Nova Scotia colony. So many loyalists came to Nova Scotia that a new colony was created, New Brunswick, on the west side of the Bay of Fundy. Many other Loyalists settled on Prince Edward Island.

A smaller number of Loyalists settled in the Quebec colony. Dissatisfied with the lack of political freedom and with Quebec's land laws, they moved into the western part of the colony and began to carve settlements out of the hardwood forests of what is now Ontario. The Upper Canada colony, as it was called in 1791, grew quickly as farms were established on the fertile soils of the Great Lakes lowlands.

The early nineteenth century was a time of struggle for the British colonies in North America. The brash new United States to the south made repeated attempts to invade Canada, with a view to annexing it. In the War of 1812, Americans were driven back several times by British troops and Canadian militia. Again, the Americans anticipated French Canadians would turn against their British rulers but the militia of Quebec vigorously protected their homeland, repelling the invaders.

British rule of Canada during this period was far from democratic, the British fearing that democracy in Canada might lead to a repetition of the American revolution. The wealthy landowners and the Anglican Church prospered at the expense of ordinary Canadians struggling to make a living on pioneer farms and in the villages of Upper and Lower Canada. A reform movement began but, frustrated by an undemocratic political process, flared into armed rebellion in 1837. The rebellions were quickly put down, but British fears that they might be repeated led to icreased political freedom in the 1840s and 1850s. Truly responsible government came first to the Nova Scotia colony and was soon followed in what was now the United Canada colony.

While the Maritimes and Canada East and Canada West were developing into communities of orderly established farms and growing towns and villages, joined by roads and rail lines, western Canada was still a true frontier zone. The rivalry between the Hudson's Bay Company and the Northwest Company had seen the creation of fur trading posts all across the west during the first half of the nineteenth century. Fur traders and explorers like Alexander Mackenzie and Simon Fraser had crossed the Rockies to the Pacific Ocean and travelled to the Arctic in search of new fur trading sites.

On the Pacific, the voyage of Captain James Cook to Nootka Sound had started a valuable trade in sea-otter pelts. The Hudson's Bay company set up trading on Vancouver Island and at Fort Langley on the banks of the Fraser River.

The great plains first seen by La Verendrye and Kelsey were slow to be settled. A Scot, Lord Selkirk, established a farming colony on the Red River in what is now Manitoba, struggling for survival alongside the Métis and Indians who still hunted buffalo and traded furs for their livelihood. Millions of square kilometres of land held by the Hudson's Bay Company covered most of the country north and west of the Canadas, little explored and even less inhabited.

Gold was discovered in British Columbia along the Fraser River in the 1850s and a great influx of miners and fortune-seekers entered the region. Many of the prospectors were Americans, drawn north by the lure of new riches after the California Gold Rush of 1849 had ended. The presence of so many Americans in the western colony alarmed the British and their Canadian subjects, causing the British to take quick action to establish the area as a colony in 1858. The American Civil War brought back memories of the war of 1812 and of American invasion attempts. Britain realized that she was ill prepared to defend six scattered colonies in North America.

At the same time, the political factions of Canada West and Canada East were locked in bitter stalemate. The only solution to all of the problems seemed to be a union of all of Britain's colonies north of the United States. The result was Confederation, a highly contentious proposal that saw Newfoundland and Prince Edward Island decide not to join with Ontario, Quebec, Nova Scotia and New Brunswick in the proposed union.

What was created on July 1, 1867 was not a new nation. Rather, it was a union of British colonies with a great degree of, but not absolute, sovereignty over their own affairs. They still depended on Britain for military and diplomatic services, two of the hallmarks of a sovereign state. But it was indeed the beginning of Canada as a modern nation.

Canada grew rapidly after Confederation. The Hudson's Bay Company lands of the northwest were purchased, and with the impetus of a Métis rebellion led by Louis Riel, the province of Manitoba was created in 1870. British Columbia joined confederation the following year, over the bitter protest of those people in Victoria who wanted to remain part of England, and of a third faction who favored union with the United States.

One of British Columbia's conditions on joining Confederation was that a railroad be built linking the isolated western province to the rest of Canada. Fourteen years passed, while the citizens of British Columbia grew restless and talked of separation from Canada, before the last spike was driven at Craigellachie in the Rocky Mountains on November 7, 1885. A few days later, the first train from Montreal reached Port Moody, and the following year, the line was extended west to Vancouver. Canada was truly a confederation from sea to sea.

Driving in the last spike, Craigellachie, B.C. 1885

The building of the railroad across Canada led quickly to the settlement of the western prairie region. Aided by a vigorous campaign to attract immigrants to Canada, the number of settlers moving onto the plains and turning grasslands into prosperous wheat farms grew steadily. These waves of immigrants, many from eastern Europe, added new pieces to the Canadian cultural mosaic beside the founding French and English tradition. Soon onion-domed orthodox churches, Doukhobour communities, Icelandic villages and black American ranchers were all part of the fabric of western Canadian society. With this rapid growth, Saskatchewan and Alberta became provinces of Canada in 1905, bringing the number to nine.

Canada during the nineteenth century had gone from a vast wilderness of pioneer farms and far-flung fur trading posts to a modern industrial nation. Fast steam locomotives spanned great distances in short periods of time. Telegraph lines joined Vancouver to Halifax, and Canada to Europe via the trans-Atlantic cable. The first commercial oil fields had been developed in Petrolia, Ontario in mid-century, and a Nova Scotia inventor, Abraham Gesner, had made the world a bright place in which to live through his development of kerosene, a petroleum by-product. By century's end, oil lamps were beginning to fade out like pioneer tallow candles as electric lights were becoming more and more common. A Canadian invention, the telephone, developed by Alexander Graham Bell in Brantford, Ontario, was offering quick and convenient communications. X-rays were being used in Canadian hospitals, and the first motor cars were on the roads.

Looking at the bright prospects of Canada on the eve of the new century, Sir Wildred Laurier said "The Twentieth Century belongs to Canada." Laurier did his best to ensure that Canada would become a strong, independent nation, gaining control over its own military and diplomatic affairs. Canada's soldiers fought bravely in World War I, but at the peace conferences and later at the League of Nations, Canada had difficulty in convincing the world that the country had a right to its own representation in world affairs.

World War I saw women begin to come into their own in Canada. Nurses during World War I were the first Canadian women to vote in a federal election. Soon, all Canadian women would be able to vote.

The economic depression of the 1930's hit Canada hard. It coincided with the great drought, when dry winds swept across the prairies, turning the bread basket of the nation into a dust bowl. Many Canadians were out of work and going to relief camps and soup kitchens for help, while others got rich selling bootleg whiskey to dry Americans in the midst of Prohibition. It was a time when bush planes and pilots like Punch Dickins and 'Wop' May were opening up Canada's northern frontier from the air, braving Arctic cold and uncharted wilderness in their fragile open aircraft. Fascism was on the rise in Europe, first in Spain where Canadians of the Mackenzie-Papineau Brigade fought with the Republican forces, and where a Canadian doctor, Norman Bethune, developed the first mobile blood transfusion service. Later, Hitler would plunge all of Europe into bloody combat. At decade's end, Canada had joined the Allied war against Germany.

War dominated the first half of the 1940's; Canadians fought in Europe, North Africa, and in Asia against the Japanese. Canada's industries geared up for the war effort, accelerating the growth of manufacturing. Women picked up rivet guns, and welding torches to aid the war effort just as men carried rifles and machine guns. Just before the war's end, Canadians celebrated the voyage of the brave and tough little RCMP vessel, the St. Roch, as it completed its voyage through the fabled northwest passage and circumnavigated North America.

As the fifties began, Canadians were fighting in Korea, but prosperity continued. The people of Canada were buying cars and household goods in unprecedented numbers, and moving their new and growing families into ranchers and bungalows in burgeoning suburbs. Television was becoming a household word. During the fifties, Canadian engineers developed and flew the world's first commercial jet airliner but the project was shelved to produce fighters for the Korean War.

The sixties were the decade in which Canadians came to be seen as peacemakers in a world of brush-fire conflicts. Lester Pearson was awarded the Nobel Peace Prize in 1957, and he worked hard as Prime Minister in the sixties to establish this country's reputation as a peaceful nation and a force for peace in the world. Canadian troops served as peace-keeping forces in Egypt, Cyprus, the Congo and other trouble spots around the world. During this time too, American draft dodgers and conscientious objectors came north to Canada, seeking to avoid their country's military involvement in Viet Nam. During the 1960's, Canada got a new flag: a distinctive, bright red, maple leaf emblem that today is instantly recognized around the world as the symbol of Canada.

The sixties had also been the time of the Quiet Revolution in Quebec, when the struggle of Québecois to feel a strong and secure sense of themselves as a distinct culture within Canada began to bear fruit. But for some, the Quiet Revolution was too quiet. The seventies began with the shock and outrage of the kidnapping of Quebec cabinet minister Pierre Laporte and British diplomat James Cross. Laporte died at the hands of his captors, Prime Minister Trudeau invoked the War Measures Act to bring the kidnappers to justice and the nation was plunged into mixed feelings of anger and despair. Despite the growing friction in the country, English and French united two years later to celebrate the victory of Team Canada over the powerful Soviet team in the 1972 Canada-Soviet Union Hockey Series.

Through the seventies Canadians enjoyed one of the world's highest standards of living, buying the best consumer goods, and enjoying the rapid growth of cultural, recreational and social services. Everyone seemed to be able to take a winter holiday in Hawaii or the Caribbean, and to be complaining about the cost of living at the same time. Quebec was in the forefront of the news throughout the seventies, but never so much as when the separatist Parti Québecois led by the charismatic René Levesque won a landslide victory in the 1976 Quebec provincial election. Canada held its breath waiting to see if Quebec would stay in Confederation, as Levesque announced that he would hold a referendum, taking the question directly to the people.

Early in 1980 it was apparent that this would be a decade of challenge and political surprises. The Federal government changed hands twice within a few months. Energy, its cost and conservation, was becoming a major consideration. Words like 'unemployment rate', 'recession' and 'inflation' were on everybody's lips. The cost of living climbed steadily, but Canada still enjoyed a standard of living and a sense of peace and security few other nations could match. The 'oui-non' debate which had raged in Quebec and across Canada was concluded in 1980. To everyone's surprise, René Levesque's Parti Québecois lost the referendum to federalist forces and the nation breathed a sigh of relief: the union stood.

The final accounting won't be in until century's end, but it appears that Laurier's vision of a strong and prosperous Canada in the twentieth century has held true. While other nations have rattled sabres and claimed greatness, Canada has quietly set about reinforcing its position as a world leader in peaceful endeavors and in developing a compassionate global consciousness, while at the same time bringing to as many of its citizens as possible peace and prosperity.

Moonlight over Lake Ontario.

58

Summer evening, St. Louis district of Montreal.

Cross country ski marathon, Lachute, Quebec.

Snow picnic, Manning Park, British Columbia.

Native Indian children, the Calgary Stampede, Alberta.

Under sail on the St. Lawrence River, Quebec City.

The waterfront, Yarmouth, Nova Scotia.

Rocky Mountain Big Horn Sheep near Canmore, Alberta.

Right: Mule Deer, Jasper National Park, Alberta.
Below: Canada Goose, Oak Hammock Marsh, Manitoba.

Above: Black Bear, Waterton Lakes, Alberta.
Right: Golden Mantled Ground Squirrel.

Following pages: Botany Bay, Vancouver Island, British Columbia.

Camping on Maligne Pass, Jasper National Park, Alberta.

The South Saskatchewan River and the City of Saskatoon.

Quebec City and the Hotel Frontenac.

The mill, Kings Landing Historical Settlement, New Brunswick.

Lake of the Woods, near Rainy River, Ontario.

Oil pump, Leduc, Alberta.

Chesterman Beach, Vancouver Island, British Columbia.

The Legislative Building, Regina, Saskatchewan.

The Montreal skyline and the St. Lawrence River.

Winter sunset near Cornwall, Ontario.

The St. Elias Range, Kluane National Park, Yukon.

Canada: The People

Quidi Vidi Pond, Newfoundland

The people of Canada are as diverse as the varied landscapes of the country itself. First peopled by native Indians and Inuit, descendents of nomadic hunters who came from Asia long ago, then founded as a nation out of the conflict of two cultures, French and English, Canada is today a nation of immigrants, a home to people from every continent and country on earth. As a people, Canadians have steadfastly resisted pressures that might have shaped them into a bland, uniform mass. Regional differences abound; each part of Canada and each group of Canadians has its own distinctive and colorful character. But, diverse as their roots may be, Canadians have a strong sense of national identity. "Canadians are generally indistinguishable from the Americans," columnist Richard Starnes once wrote, "and the surest way of telling the two apart is to make the observation to a Canadian."

Unity in diversity is the hallmark of the Canadian people. Canada is a nation and a people with two official languages, no common religion, and a few shared traditions and experiences. The people of Canada have, for the most part, agreed to accept the diversity of their nation and to build within it. The fact that Canada is a parliamentary democracy helps sustain this pluralism. Multiculturalism, the open recognition and celebration of the many races and cultures who have come together to shape Canada, is the official policy of the Canadian government.

Canadians are often thought of as those immigrants who arrived in the land sometime after the 15th or 16th century and stayed to settle it. But the first Canadians arrived here many thousands of years before that time. They were natives of Asia who followed migrating herds of animals across the polar ice cap, and then south. The story of these first migrants goes so far back in the memory of mankind that it has been lost in the mists of time and is thought of as a time of the creator. A native chief speaks of his people's beginnings: "God created the Indian country, and it was like he spread out a big blanket. He put Indians on it. They were created here in this country, truly honest, and that was the time this river started to run. When we were created we were given our ground to live on and from this time these were our rights. I was not brought here from a foreign country and did not come here. I was put here by the creator."

These first Canadians had a culture and an identity which is only now being rediscovered. In Old Crow, a village on the Porcupine River in the Yukon Territory, archaeological digs found man made implements which carbon dating has indicated to be 25,000 years old, the oldest evidence of man in North America. In his book *Saskatchewan*, Edward McCourt writes, "Troy town rose and fell ten times on the hill Hissarlik above the Hellespont; the Indian village sited a few miles west of Moose Jaw went Troy three better — thirteen distinct cultural levels have been uncovered in the Mortlach midden."

For 25,000 years or more these people developed a way of life in harmony with nature, evolving and changing, creating art and societal structures. It all changed radically when the European 'discoverers' arrived.

The first Europeans who arrived on the eastern shore of the New Found Land had come from an exhausted Europe, from economic slavery, from a time of broken faith and persecution. In fleeing from these things, they were also leaving behind centuries of civilization. Many arrived in the wilderness with only their memories and what few material goods they could carry. On arrival, they did not find the land of gold and riches they anticipated. They found instead a savagely beautiful wilderness, rich in resources and wealthy in promise for those with vision, and for those who could survive. They hacked out their homesteads in the forests and built a life on the basis of that promise. These first settlers, and the hopeful immigrants who came in ever-increasing numbers, were from a great variety of backgrounds. These cultural streams flowed into a common pool, forming a distinctively Canadian identity, often described as a cultural mosaic.

Canada is a patchwork quilt of cultures and races, in contrast to the so-called "melting pot" of other nations of recent immigrants such as Australia, New Zealand, or the United States. Stroll along the main street of any major Canadian city, drive through the vast countryside, and the colourful pieces of this great Canadian mosaic will come into clear focus.

Start with a walk along Vancouver's Robson Street, known locally as Robson-strasse because of the many German shops that line its sidewalks. In a few short blocks it is possible to hear every European language spoken. Sit in a sidewalk cafe or a konditorei, eat some strudel or Black Forest cake, drink an espresso, and watch the faces of Canada stroll by. Less than a kilometre away is Chinatown with its savoury cuisine and exotic shops, where crowds of every nationality jostle elbow to elbow at green-grocers' stands which sell fresh produce from Fraser Valley farms. To the west of Vancouver's downtown is a busy Greek community, whose restaurants and bars are the social centres of the community, and where Vancouverites of all cultural backgrounds gather to meet and eat. East of the city's core lies Little Italy, where recent immigrants from Italy and Portugal now occupy Victorian homes that two generations ago housed Scottish masons and carpenters, at that time themselves newcomers to Canada.

Vancouver is striking proof of the fact that Canada is a nation of immigrants. One out of two residents of the city was born outside of Canada. The friendly babel of many languages in Vancouver arises from the fact that one-third of all Vancouverites have as their native tongue a language other than English.

Drive along the broad straight highways of the vast fertile Prairies. Here evidence of past waves of immigration to Canada stand against the wide sky. The great onion-domed silhouettes of Orthodox churches, places of worship for Ukrainians and other Eastern Europeans whose settler forefathers stepped off the newly-built Canadian Pacific Railroad nearly one hundred years ago, can be seen across Western Canada. They came to farm the tough Prairie grasslands, and to escape poverty and religious persecution in their homelands. The long highway will take you through small towns where names like Edberg and New Norway and white-washed Lutheran churches reflect the hard-working Scandinavian folk who settled there.

Visit the Calgary Stampede and you'll find black ranchers, Indian rodeo riders, and Ukrainian chuckwagon racers, along with cowboys whose sun and wind-darkened faces hide the fact that they are the great-grandsons of English and Scottish aristocrats.

Follow the highways past Mormon temples, whose congregations came north from the United States; travel past old Catholic churches in French communities whose founders came west with the fur trade. Stop in a small Prairie town where Hutterite farmers in nineteenth century clothes come to shop on Saturday. Have a bowl of borscht and some good kosher smoked meat or fish in Winnipeg before boarding a train for Toronto.

Nowhere does the patchwork of Canadian multi-culturalism show its bright colours so vividly as in Toronto's Kensington Market. Here you can find goods and people from every part of the world. Enter the market and you are quickly swept along in a swirling, laughing, talking mixture of many languages, skin colours and styles of dress. Listen closely and you can hear Swahili, Croatian, Hungarian, Spanish, or Arabic being spoken. Sounds of reggae, fado and Italian lovesongs pour from shops along the market street as you move from place to place, entering first a Dutch cheese shop, then an East Indian spice store, a West Indian fish store, an Italian coffee shop, a Portuguese butcher shop, or a Chinese green-grocery. Stop at a small cafe in the market and have some falafal, an Arab dish from the Middle East and reflect on the cultural kaleidoscope passing by the window. Faced with the sounds, colours and harmony of so many different groups of people shopping together in the market, it is hard to imagine Toronto as the aloof bastion of English Canada it once was.

A short flight takes you to Montreal and a visit to that cosmopolitan city's "Old Town", where the sounds of traditional Québecois folksongs drift from open doors and strolling street musicians. Somewhere a fiddle strikes up a lively jig, a reminder of the time when Catholic Irish immigrants came to work in the forests and sawmills of the Ottawa and Saguenay river valleys, mixing and marrying among the French and sharing with them their lively dance tunes. The ancient stone buildings of the old town are reminders that French Canadians have been here longer than any other group except the native Indians.

The French colonists were the first to carry the name Canadians. Jacques Cartier named the lands along the St. Lawrence River 'Canada' when he mistook the Indian word for village, "kanata," for the native's name for their homeland. For years following the British conquest of New France, the people of Quebec proudly called themselves Canadiens as a symbol of their ties to the new land and to clearly set themselves aside from the British settlers whose loyalties they felt lay far across the Atlantic. The proud and defiant cry of the Sons of Liberty during the Rebellion of 1837 was "Avant tout je suis Canadien" — "Before all else I am a Canadian."

The people of Atlantic Canada have roots that go deep in Canada's history; this region was explored and settled even before the founding of Quebec on the St. Lawrence River. Here there are strong traces of all of Canada's founding cultures, preserved by pride and by relative isolation from the mainstream of life in more cosmopolitan areas of Canada. In small fishing villages and isolated farming communities Highland Scots still speak Gaelic, while the Acadian residents of New Brunswick speak the French of the first settlers of Atlantic Canada. On Prince Edward Island or in Newfoundland, the lilt of Irish accents the speech of people whose families first came to the islands as many as eight generations ago. In Nova Scotia the skirl of bagpipes can be heard and kilted dancers and athletes compete at the annual Highland Games. An early summer visit to a fishing village may find you caught up in the procession as the local bishop blesses the fishing fleet before the start of another season. At Halifax or

Dartmouth there are blacks whose ancestors came to the region as slaves owned by Loyalist refugees 200 years ago.

From this multicultural mosaic there has emerged a sense of union, a oneness in being Canadian. This is most evident in the churches of Canada. When Jacques Cartier landed on the Gaspé coast and planted a 10-metre high cross he was claiming the land not only for France but for his faith. The settlers who came after him followed a similar pattern. The first community building erected in any settlement was the church, a link with the past symbolizing the faith that had brought them to this new land. As groups became established, they united and found strength in numbers, sometimes casting off old structures and rewriting the rules in keeping with the fresh perspective of their new home.

This restructuring was most dramatic in Protestant churches which departed from tradition to create truly Canadian churches. All branches of the Methodists united into one Canadian Methodist church and all Congregationalists formed one union. Presbyterians, with a small dissenting minority, followed suit. In 1925 these three combined to form the United Church of Canada, the first such union in Protestant history.

The Roman Catholic church had built a strong base in French Canada as the country was settled, and governed satellite parishes from there. Today 51% of the country is Catholic. Roman Catholic, Anglican and United Church congregations combined make up 80% of the population of Canada. The remainder is made up of a group of smaller denominations as diverse as the lands from which Canadians have come.

Eskimo Family, ice fishing.

BARB·WOOD

As churches were a symbol of settlers' faith so did they become a focal point for cultural activities. New immigrants usually gravitated to an area where their culture was identifiable and where they could worship in their own faith. Farmers broke and settled the land, merchants arrived to supply their needs, pastor, teacher, doctor, more business and finally bureaucrats to administer government programs arrived. Gradually the face of the community changed, but usually the churches remained central to community life.

This aspect of the church remains as true for immigrants today as it was a century ago. New Canadians are often faced with a language they do not understand, signs they cannot read and food they are unaccustomed to. Their church can have a supportive function while inducting them into the new society.

In Vancouver, a small French Canadian cultural centre is focused around a church; a Muslim community in Edmonton worships at the mosque of Al Rashid; Hutterites live in communal villages on the prairies, and Doukhobours farm in British Columbia. In Toronto, Italian immigrants have made their own lively space in the city, and in Vancouver there is the largest Chinese sector north of San Francisco. Winnipeg still mirrors the many cultures that grew around the old fur trading post of Fort Garry: The Métis, French, natives, Scots, Irish, British and more recently the Ukrainians.

These communities relive and remember their heritage, history, traditional occupations and sports in festivals that sing the song of Canada. Each year the Calgary Stampede revives the romance of the west with chuckwagon racing, bull riding and bronco bustin'. The Raftsmen's Festival at Hull, Quebec brings back memories of the great rafts of logs which once came from the white pine forests. Icelandic, Ukrainian and Norwegian festivals are held across the prairies. Edmonton recreates the goldrush era with Klondike Days and Kamloops, British Columbia, remembers a group of goldseekers in Overlander Days. The Sourdough Rendezvous in Whitehorse, Yukon Territory, recreates a time not long past with dogsled racing, flour packing and Mad Trapper events that last a week. The Quebec Winter Carnival recreates scenes from the past with modern sporting events and the Sea Festival in Vancouver celebrates that city's link to the sea. Here at these festivals, Canadians celebrate their past, and in doing so they affirm the present and future of this proudly multicultural nation.

This cultural diversity is united in Canada, providing an identity reflected by names known the world over: Banting and Best, Hans Selye, Karen Kain, Lynn Seymour, Jon Vickers, Cunard, Mordecai Richler, Farley Mowat, Pierre Berton, Margaret Lawrence, Margaret Atwood, Norman Bethune, Marshall McLuhan, Alexander Graham Bell, Norman Jewison, Donald Sutherland, Mary Pickford, Raymond Massey, Raymond Burr, Lorne Greene, Christopher Plummer, Walter Pidgeon, Gordon Lightfoot, Anne Murray, Joni Mitchell, Leonard Cohen, Arthur Erikson, Lester Pearson, Stephen Leacock, Emily Carr, Moe Koffman, Jay Silverheels, Guy Lombardo, Oscar Peterson,

William Kurelek, Gilles Villenueve, Wayne Gretzky, Bobby Orr, Nancy Greene, Barbara Ann Scott, Chief Dan George and Lord Thompson of Fleet.

But ethnic backgrounds and individual achievements alone do not tell us who the Canadian people are. There is more to being a Canadian than bringing an old culture to a new land, or in achieving recognition. A major factor in the development of the Canadian personality has been the relationship of the people to the land, with its vast landscapes, its wild beauty and great natural resources.

Hollywood has seized on this relationship between Canadians and their magnificent northern environment, and distorted it. On the screen, Canadians appear as mad trappers, lonely fur traders, tough lumberjacks and occasionally as romantic singing mounties.

There are indeed trappers who tend lonely northern traplines and whose rich harvests of furs grace high fashion salons the world over, but their dogsleds and rough pine bough shelters have been replaced by snowmobiles and prefab houses. Strong fallers and buckers still bring down the tall trees of Canada's forests, using chainsaws and skidders that make their still hazardous task a little easier than the days when pioneer loggers cut massive Douglas firs with two man crosscut saws. The Mounties, both men and women, still patrol most of Canada's great distances but their horses appear only in ceremonial parades. Today, aircraft, computers, and other modern technologies help them police the world's second largest country. Helicopters and remote-sensing space satellites aid geologists and prospectors to add to Canada's already great storehouse of minerals and energy resources, yet there remain the strong, lone ones who put gold pans and rock hammers into their backpacks and head into the hills seeking their fortunes. There are the brave and sturdy workers who go deep below the earth's surface to draw out its mineral wealth and send it on its way to the smelters and factories of Canada's industrial centres. There is the Prairie farmer who works in an air-conditioned, stereo-equipped tractor, no less weather beaten, no farther from the soil than his father's father, who rode a horse-drawn reaper over the same fields. And there are the fishermen who dare the grey and stormy seas in boats large and small, bringing in rich catches from some of the world's finest fisheries.

As city dwellers, Canadians are skilled and sophisticated workers too. They are loggers, trappers, farmers, miners, and fishermen, but they are also designers of space satellite telecommunication systems, computer specialists, builders of aircraft and automobiles, nuclear research scientists. They are concert pianists, filmmakers, ballet dancers, football players, and fashion models. Bankers and lawyers are as much a part of resource development in Canada today as the backpack and goldpan were to miners who crossed the Chilcoot Pass into the Yukon.

Canadians depend on the land and its resources for their well-being; without it, they would not enjoy their comfortable affluence, one of the highest standards of living in the world. But the relationship is deeper, more subtle and more complex than that.

Poets, novelists and artists, who draw their inspiration from Canada's many land-scapes, have been fascinated by the magic of the land. Some, like the Group of Seven and Emily Carr, have gained international fame for their powerful celebrations of Canada's natural beauty. Pacific and Atlantic coasts, Arctic islands, the rocks of the Canadian Shield and the broad expanses of the Prairies have all touched the artist's heart. And there are many fine native Indian and Inuit artists and carvers who have maintained traditional art forms, capturing the spirit of the land and its animal inhabitants in striking designs.

Few Canadians today are confronted with the harsh realities of their environment as the early settlers were, but they are still affected deeply by the vast and overwhelming nature of the landscape. The wilderness that begins at the doorstep of virtually every Canadian city has remained central to the Canadian identity. The land has shaped and informed the consciousness of the people: its size, its loneliness, its power and its sheer beauty. Despite or perhaps because of this, Canadians today are largely an urban people; 80% live in cities. One quarter of all Canadians live in two cities, Toronto and Montreal. Of the total population, 35% live in Ontario and 28% in Quebec. At 25 million people Canadians total 0.6% of the world's population living on 7% of the world's land area. This means that there is an immense amount of unsettled, unpopulated and even unexplored land. A great deal of this territory is now undergoing exploration for resource development and scientific purposes, but there is also a growing awareness of the need to preserve the land in its natural state.

From the time when settlers were faced with the overwhelming task of wrestling homesteads from the impenetrable forests of the new land, to today, when it has become important to preserve those forests for generations to come, the Canadian people have been growing and shaping themselves into a nation. The country began as diverse, often divisive, groups of people who were often forced to band together for survival. Canada has grown through rebellions, minor conflicts and a war with the United States, to take its place as a nation in world conflicts. It has been said that during the first great war Canada earned her stripes. Brigadier General Alexander Ross said of the men at Vimy Ridge in World War I, "It was Canada from the Atlantic to the Pacific on parade. I thought then, and I think today, that in those few minutes I witnessed the birth of a nation."

Canada has taken the role of peacemaker on the world stage, becoming known as a nation which puts diplomacy before conflict. This is perhaps an outgrowth of the formation of the country: a nation born of conflict and diversity. Canadians have agreed to accept that diversity and to build with it.

Kenneth Boulding, an American, summed up Canada thus: "Canada has no cultural unity, no linguistic unity, no religious unity, no economic unity, no geographic unity. All it has is unity." That unity resides in the Canadian people.

Totem pole, Prince Rupert, British Columbia.

The boardwalk, Point Pelee National Park, Ontario.

Mount Columbia, the highest peak in Alberta.

Ships leaving the Welland Canal, Lake Erie, Ontario.

Castle Mountain and the Bow River, Alberta.

The St. John River Valley, New Brunswick.

Abandoned farmhouse, Prince Edward Island.

St. Joseph's Oratory, Montreal, Quebec.

Prairie winter, Meacham, Saskatchewan.

Midnight skyline, Eskimo Point, Hudson Bay.

Following pages: the Houses of Parliament and the Ottawa River, Ottawa, Ontario.

87

Near Abbotsford, British Columbia.

Ukrainian Church, Winnipeg, Manitoba.

Mountain Goat, Jasper National Park, Alberta.

Mount Sir Donald, Glacier National Park, British Columbia.

Rosseau Falls, Muskoka, Ontario.

Ice floes near Pangnirtung, Baffin Island.

Boats in a quiet inlet on Galiano Island, British Columbia.

Falls near Corner Brook, Newfoundland.

Maritime sunset in the Bay of Fundy.